If you don't read this book
you ought to be ashamed of yourself.
If you do - you will be.

Do you wish to see the world?

Go to the airport
- or the optician.

God is a DJ
He doesn't do requests

I wanted wine, women and song.
I got a drunk woman singing.

ex.
If you want it badly
that's how you're
going to get it

He who binds to himself a joy
doth the winged life destroy.
But he who kisses the joy as it flies
lives in Eternity's sunrise

William Blake

He who lives in Eternity's sunrise
Is seldom inspired to do the washing up

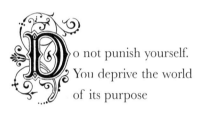

o not punish yourself.
You deprive the world
of its purpose

Life is unfair
most admit when pressed
even those doing the pressing
sometimes agree
but is life so unfair
we need a lottery
as well as a justice system?

You can make many interesting things out of matchsticks

But not an oak

If a million monkies were given a million typewriters, eventually one of them might produce the complete works of Shakespeare but to reach it would it be worth wading through four hundred thousand copies of "Money" by Martin Amis?

The rolling stone
may gather
no moss

But it can start
an avalanche

I am a security guard
I have some security guard jokes for you:

How many security guards does
it take to change a lightbulb?
One. We're not stupid.

Three Security Guards go into a pub.
Nothing happens. But that's what we get paid for.

A steel door with two yale locks and a reinforced safety chain.
Not so funny that one but extremely secure.

Knock knock. Who's there?
Just checking.

Why did the chicken cross the road?
I can't tell you: Security.

The social life is good, we have our own club
"The Security Guard Club".
It used to have a more continental sounding name
"Club Security Guard"
but some took that a bit too literally.

It has a motto written above the door:
The watched pot may never boil
But it doesn't get nicked neither

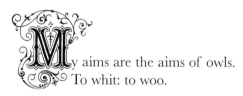**M**y aims are the aims of owls.
To whit: to woo.

Eh ladies?

I don't worry about losing my looks.

It's finding them on someone else that worries me.

ehind every great man there
lies a great woman.
And one in front of him
as well if he's lucky.

Whatever it says in the Bible
the truth remains
You can read the Bible and dismiss
it as nonsense if you like;
you can dismiss it as nonsense without
reading it to save time if you prefer

BIG J SON OF G

I often compare myself to Jesus.
I've come to the conclusion
I'm not as good.
But whatever you think of him now,
if you were there at the time you would
probably have found him irritating.
For example he repeatedly said
"stop what you're doing and follow me –
you are fishermen I shall make you
fishers of men; you are carpenters
I shall make you carpenters of men –
surgeons – but stop what you are doing
and follow me". Until right at the end
when he said "You can't follow me
any more I'm going to my Dad's. Bye!"
At one point someone says to him
"I would follow you lord but my father
has just died and I have to bury him"
And Jesus uttered the immortal line
"Let the dead bury their dead!".
If you were there at the time you
might have found it a little insensitive,
as well as impractical.

And when he said "Who by taking
thought can add one cubit to his
stature?" I wish I'd been there because
I'd have said "What about stilts?"

When you look in the mirror in despair and none of your clothes seem appropriate, don't worry, relax, put the kettle on: it might suit you. And in any case when one is wearing a kettle the rest of ones clothes seldom attract comment.

The truly beautiful
are often abused
for apparent ugliness
just as those with great vision
often bump into things.

Without a deadline
I do nothing
With a deadline
I do nothing
Until the deadline is upon me
Then I panic
Which is doing nothing quickly
When the deadline has passed
I begin work
On my excuses.

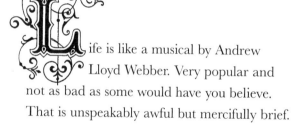ife is like a musical by Andrew Lloyd Webber. Very popular and not as bad as some would have you believe. That is unspeakably awful but mercifully brief.

He who disagrees with me in private, call him a fool.

He who disagrees with me in public, call him an ambulance.

In love as in fighting
the winner has an
eight foot pole.

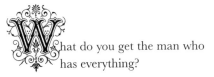

What do you get the man who has everything?

Might I suggest a gravestone enscribed with the words: so what?

My dog has no legs.

Yet still he chews bones.

How does a dog with no legs chew bones?

With a great deal of suspicion

I've noticed.

All men are brothers.
Hence war.

Look at the sea
and remember the past.
Look at the sky
and imagine the future.
Look at the land
and think of the present.

And at the most profound place
where land, sea and sky are one -
there ye shall play volleyball.

You can't fool
all of the people
all of the time.
But you can try.

It's called
advertising.

Dangerous Things

- Matches
- Golf balls moving at high speed
- Doors marked W.C. that just have
  a huge drop on the other side
- Very heavy weights suspended above your head
  by a piece of cotton
- Microwave ovens that sing to you
  "Come put your head inside and turn me on"
- Cars driven by idiots
- Cars driven by very sensible people swerving
  to avoid cars driven by idiots
- Cars driven by policemen
  chasing cars driven by idiots
- Policemen generally; they're dangerous.
  It is universally agreed by all policemen
  that the police have an impossible job to do.
  Nevertheless they insist on attempting to do it.
  This leads to frustration.
- Scissors that move of the own accord.
  And attempt to cut your genitals off - if
  you are male that is, as everybody should be.

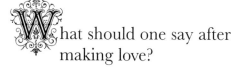

What should one say after making love?

Thank you seems too much.
I'm sorry - not enough.

I remember when I posed
as a customs officer so that
I could meet Oscar Wilde.
I said to him "Have you
anything to declare?"
He said "I have nothing
to declare but my genius."
I said "I'll put that down
as nothing then shall I?"

The electric guitar
- like making love -
    is much improved by a little feedback,
    completely ruined by too much.

Many drink to forget.
Few forget to drink

He who lives by the sword,
shall die by the sword.
Indeed - likewise he who
lives by the pen, he who lives
by the word processor,
he who who lives by
the fax machine -
all shall die by the sword.
Only he who lives by the tank
shall remain immune.

"Brevity is the soul of wit"
said Shakespeare.
I say "Wank!" Thus I win.

I could've been a boxer.
Like my father.
He could've been a boxer as well.
I come from a long line of men who
could've been boxers.
If only we'd taken any interest in boxing.
Or learned how to box.

en lie.

Women wear
perfume and makeup
And lie.

I decree that history shall be rewritten.

This time without any punctuation so that it is just one sentence linked together by the phrase "And then what happened was..."

reatness sits upon my shoulders as the dog urinates upon the pavement - with naturalness and ease and some offence to passers-by.

It is said that at the age of 55 each man becomes what he most despised at the age of 25.

I live in constant fear lest I become a badly organised trip to Bournemouth.

Have you anything to say?
No? Then shut up.
Unless you are a woman
in which case carry on
- it's delightful.

LONDON

The city that goes to bed quite late

Parable of the cockneys

In the beginning was the word
Hearing of this the cockneys
wondered what it might rhyme with
and whether it was worth nicking
And god so loved the world
he gave his only son
Hearing of this the cockneys
called everyone son
Because they like the sound of it
And it made them feel a bit like God

And God so loved the cockneys
he gave them London to live in
And Essex to dream of
Life was nasty brutish and short
And so were the cockneys
They had not much food and
would even look in dustbins for
something to eat and if they found
a dead cat they would eat it but they
did not regard a dead cat as a treat
and this raised them above the scousers

Plagarism is the highest form of art just as theft is the highest form of commerce.

It is the vanity
of women
to spend hours
in front
of the mirror.
It is the vanity
of men
not to bother.

I wear glasses.
As an affectation,
as a badge of high
intellect and also
to see with.

Cleanliness is next to godliness.
And the chip shop
is next to the hair dresser's.
It doesn't persuade
me to visit either.

Inside every naked woman there is a fully clothed one trying to get out

- but what to wear?

Like most supermodels,
I won't get out of bed
for less than £3000.
Unlike most supermodels,
I don't get out of bed very often.

If you only ever read
one book in your life

I highly recommend you
keep your mouth shut

Rules for conversing with a potential suicide bomber

1. Be polite, but firm.
2. Resist the temptation to discuss your own problems.

To the Italians I say this
"Rome wasn't built in a day.
Perhaps it could have been
if you spoke less with your arms"

A million monkeys
were given a million typewriters.
It's called the internet.

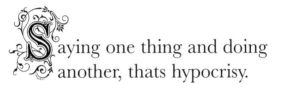 Saying one thing and doing another, thats hypocrisy.

Saying many things and doing nothing, that's democracy

The rules for making love to a woman

1. Don't, you fool:
   Why stoke the volcano of grief?

What a lot of people don't realise
is that if you look at things globally,
from a strictly economic perspective,
that makes you a wanker.

I have the
brain of an
eagle, the heart
of a lion, the
engorged
member of
a rampant
hippopotomus:
All I need now
is some glue.

Naturally all marriages end in disaster. Death, divorce or of course, marriage.

Why do men die before
their wives?
Could it be because
they want to?

You can only glimpse true misery in hot weather - everything else is simply absence of sun. Likewise you can only glimpse true loneliness when surrounded by friends - everything else is simply absence of friends.

If you wish to experience the truest misery and loneliness possible, it follows that you must gather your family and friends and go to some warm and beautiful place. You could call it a holiday.

There is a better sport than Javelin: Discus.

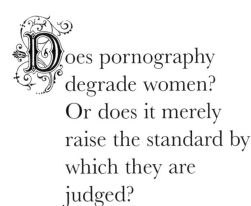

Does pornography degrade women? Or does it merely raise the standard by which they are judged?

Perhaps it was women who invented kissing - to stop men's mouths.

Recently I conceived an ambition.
I wish to be the first person to
reach the South Pole. Accidentally.

It was only after my father showed me what I would inherit that I struggled to keep him alive.

There must be many things
that we don't have words for,
can anyone think of one?

I was walking down the road the other day, and I couldn't help but notice how beautiful the world is. And I thought to myself "Why would anyone in their right mind bother to take drugs?". Then I remembered I was on drugs, and that was the reason.

Remember in Russia
Nostalgia is regarded
as an illness so they say

Or rather it used to be
In the good old days

Like most true Scots I secretly loath
the haggis the kilt and the caber.
Unlike most true Scots I'm not Scottish.

Your importance in this world
is incalculable.
Now get some sleep

You will never defeat us
For we have already defeated ourselves

IN THE END
ALL THAT MATTERS
IS WHAT YOU PASS ON.

PASS IT ON.